CELTIC VECTOR DESIGNS

CELTIC VECTOR DESIGNS

DOVERPICTURA

DOVER PUBLICATIONS, INC. | Mineola, New York

By Alan Weller.
Designed by Joel Waldrep.

Celtic Vector Designs is a new work, first published by Dover Publications, Inc.,
in 2008.

The CD-ROM file names correspond to the images in the book. All of the artwork
stored on the CD-ROM can be imported directly into a wide range of design and
word-processing programs on either Windows or Macintosh platforms. No further
installation is necessary.

ISBN 10: 0-486-99022-2
ISBN 13: 978-0-486-99022-4
Manufactured in the United States of America
Dover Publications, Inc., 31 East 2nd Street, Mineola, NY 11501
www.doverpublications.com

GALLERY—PAGES 1, 2, 4, 8 thru 29

Provides you with examples, from basic to complex, of compositions designed using vectors and textures from the accompanying CD. On the right-hand side of each pair of pages is an 'asset panel,' in which you will find a listing of all of the components and colors that were used in the creation of the illustrations.

TUTORIALS—PAGES 30 thru 51

Contains instructional materials pertaining to the examples shown in the Gallery section of this book. Use this section to learn how work with vector images and to create your own compositions in Adobe Illustrator. These tutorials will teach you about basic elements such as shapes, paths, and anchor points, and will give you step-by-step instructions for coloring, reshaping, scaling and patterning.

VECTORS—PAGES 52 thru 127

Shows simple, clean renderings of all of the vector images that are on the accompanying CD.

WHAT'S ON THE CD

EPS and SVG vector files of all of the images in the Vectors section.
JPG bit-mapped files of all of the images in the Vectors section.
EPS vector files of all of the vector textures used in the Gallery section.
JPG files of all of the bitmap textures used in the Gallery section.
JPG files of all of the illustrations in the Gallery section of the book.
Dover Design Manager

SOFTWARE AND HARDWARE REQUIREMENTS

The vector images on the included CD are suitable for use on computers running Windows 98, 2000, XP or Vista; or Macintosh OS 9.1–OS X. The computer should have sufficient RAM to power the type of graphics software program with which these image files are intended for use; 256MB minimum, 512MB recommended.

To fully utilize these vector images they must be used with an illustration program such as Adobe Illustrator®, Macromedia Freehand®, or Corel Draw®, or a web animation program such as Adobe Flash®. The images can also be opened, but with limited functionality, in pixel image-editing programs such as Adobe Photoshop®, Adobe Photoshop Elements®, and Corel PaintShop®. This book and CD does not contain any of the above software.

163

016

097

165

VT 010

Techniques Used:
Fill, Outline, Gradient, Scale,
Flip, Rotate

	10c	20m	100y	0k
	0c	50m	10y	70k
	40c	50m	40y	30k

	225r	203g	0b
	95r	59g	66b
	126r	101g	101b

237

096

006

256

VT 008

BT 005

Techniques Used:
Fill, Outline, Gradient, Drop Shadow,
Repetition, Clipping Mask, Scale,
Flip, Rotate

	60c	20m	20y	20k
	40c	20m	30y	20k
	10c	10m	30y	10k
	100r	141g	159b
	141r	154g	148b
	216r	208g	174b

135

076

220

253

VT 001

BT 007

BT 010

Techniques Used:
Fill, Outline, Gradient, Repetition,
Clipping Mask, Scale, Flip, Rotate

	10c	0m	60y	0k
	10c	20m	100y	0k
	0c	90m	80y	10k

	229r	227g	102b
	231r	171g	0b
	200r	39g	42b

257

239

233

241

248

VT 004

BT 002

BT 003

Techniques Used:
Fill, Outline, Gradient, Repetition,
Clipping Mask, Scale, Flip, Rotate

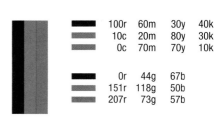

	100r	60m	30y	40k
	10c	20m	80y	30k
	0c	70m	70y	10k
	0r	44g	67b	
	151r	118g	50b	
	207r	73g	57b	

15

067

133

080   092

102

VT 011

BT 004

Techniques Used:
Fill, Outline, Gradient, Drop Shadow,
Repetition, Clipping Mask,
Scale, Flip, Rotate

	70c	0m	50y	0k
	50c	20m	100y	0k
	60c	0m	60y	60k

	14r	155g	125b
	116r	138g	37b
	37r	70g	52b

261

138

252

151

025

010

VT 005

Techniques Used:
Fill, Outline, Gradient, Drop Shadow,
Repetition, Scale, Flip, Rotate

	50c	0m	100y	0k
	0c	50m	10y	70k
	40c	50m	60y	40k
	10c	10m	30y	0k
	125r	198g	34b	
	95r	59g	66b	
	110r	88g	69b	
	234r	225g	198b	

014

068

244

VT 002

Techniques Used:
Fill, Outline, Gradient, Drop Shadow,
Repetition, Scale, Flip, Rotate

40c	0m	10y	0k
20c	0m	100y	0k
10c	0m	40y	0k
20c	0m	10y	0k

146r	214g	227b
205r	208g	10b
223r	229g	142b
158r	215g	215b

164

012

004

262

VT 007

BT 008   BT 013   BT 011

Techniques Used:
Fill, Outline, Gradient, Drop Shadow,
Clipping Mask, Scale

0c	40m	70y	0k
0c	20m	50y	0k
10c	10m	40y	10k
10c	10m	50y	30k
254r	134g	71b	
255r	182g	110b	
193r	173g	121b	
147r	131g	86b	

23

224

267

247

269

VT 011

Techniques Used:
Fill, Outline, Gradient, Drop Shadow,
Repetition, Scale, Flip

	0c	90m	80y	10k
	20c	30m	80y	30k
	60c	0m	30y	30k
	10c	20m	100y	0k
	200r	39g	42b	
	131r	101g	49b	
	31r	113g	111b	
	231r	171g	0b	

25

064

077

087

070

066

VT 003

BT 014

Techniques Used:
Fill, Outline, Gradient, Repetition
Clipping Mask, Scale, Flip, Rotate

	100c	60m	30y	40k
	60c	0m	30y	30k
	10c	10m	80y	20k
	10c	0m	60y	0k

	0r	44g	67b
	31r	113g	111b
	177r	150g	56b
	229r	227g	102b

240

082

231

003

083

VT 006

Techniques Used:
Fill, Outline, Gradient, Repetition,
Scale, Flip, Rotate

	70c	50m	30y	40k
	0c	5m	40y	0k
	0c	50m	80y	10k
	10c	20m	50y	0k
	68r	77g	97b	
	254r	241g	174b	
	222r	144g	60b	
	231r	206g	143b	

About These Tutorials

The following are basic instructional tutorials for the techniques used to create the illustrations within the Gallery section of this book. These illustrations were created using Adobe Illustrator, and a basic working knowledge of this program is important to mastering these techniques. More in-depth information about this program can be found under the Adobe Illustrator Help tab, or by visiting the Adobe website at www.adobe.com.

These tutorials have been performed using the Macintosh version of Adobe Illustrator CS2. If you have a newer or older version of Illustrator, some variation could occur in how your software displays the tools used in these tutorials. Also, there are minor differences in functionality and nomenclature between the Windows and Macintosh versions of Illustrator. Consult your Illustrator manual or the Help tab if you do not find the Tool, Window, Menu, or Palette described in the tutorial.

Opening Vectors in Illustrator

1. On the top menu bar, go to the drop-down menu File>Open.

2. In the Open Window, locate the Dover CD which is in your computer's CD drive, double click.

3. Double click on the 'Images' folder

4. Double click on the subfolder that contains the image that you wish to open.

5. Double click on the vector file that you wish to open.

Some Basics about Vectors

Unlike bit-mapped images which are composed of pixels, vector graphics use points, lines, and curves to define shapes. Because of this they are 'resolution independent,' and can be reshaped, scaled, or resized without a loss of image quality. Please note that the final quality of your image will be determined by the resolution of your printer, or when viewing on-screen, by the quality of your monitor.

1. A vector 'path' can either be open (like the curved line) or closed (like the circle).

2. Paths are made up of segments that create the entire shape. Each segment is defined by anchor points. Anchor points can be corner points or smooth points; points can be manipulated using direction lines to change the curvature of the segment.

Selection Tool (V)

Rotate Tool (R)

Scale Tool (S)

Shear Tool

Reflect Tool (O)

Fill (X)

Stroke

This is a list of the basic tools used in the tutorials. If the Tool bar is not displayed it can be accessed from the top menu bar by going Window>Tools. The Tool bar is extremely handy, and gives quick access to the basic design tools. Some variant tools are hidden from view, and can be accessed by clicking and holding down the mouse over a related tool's icon. Tools with variants have small arrows in the bottom right hand corner of their icon.

To learn more about the Tool bar, search under the Help tab, or in the manual that accompanied your software.

This is a list of the basic Palettes used in the tutorials. Most palettes can be accessed from the top menu bar by going Window>Palettes.
Please note that in Adobe Illustrator Palettes can also be referred to as Windows.

Swatches Palette

Layers Palette

Gradient Palette

Transform Palette

Align Palette

Most of the vector images contained in this book come from rare, old sources. In creating these vectors we have tried to maintain the unique intrinsic qualities of the original artwork, while imbuing them with all of the utility that the vector file format affords. Generally, the images in this publication are of two types: regular, closed-cell illustrations which can be 'released' into individual, manipulable shapes; and more expressive, "hand-drawn" illustrations. Please note that because of the complex nature of the latter, the best results in working with this type of image require a fast computer with large allocation of RAM. The simplest method for making more RAM available to Adobe Illustrator is to shut down all unnecessary software programs.

The expressive potential of compositions made with vector images is limitless. In addition to print layouts they can be used to create silkscreen stencils, embroidery patterns, or signage designs to be cut in vinyl. They can be combined with bit-mapped images, used as paths along which type can be flowed, or as texture in multilayered compositions. Vectors tend to be relatively small files, and work very well with programs that generate web graphics, such as Adobe Flash and Fireworks. We encourage you to experiment with these images and to be creative!

TUTORIALS

1

2

3

4

5

1. Select the image using the Selection Tool found at the top left corner of the tool bar [V]. A box will appear around the image.

2. Grab one of the corners of the box and drag it out diagonally to enlarge it. To reduce the image, drag it in. To scale the image proportionally, hold down the shift key while dragging.

3. Enlarged image.

4. You can also enlarge the image with the Transform Palette. Click the chain icon at the right of the palette to link the width and height together and scale proportionally.

5. To scale proportionally, enter either the desired width or height. To scale non-proportionally, both width and height must be entered.

6. Try the Scale Tool [S] found in the tool bar to achieve similar results.

1 **2** **3** **4**

1. Select the image using the Selection Tool found at the top left corner of the tool bar [V].

2. On the top menu bar, go to the drop-down menu Window>Transform to open the Transform Palette. Click on the arrow next to the rotate input field at the lower left of the palette.

3. Select the desired angle from the pop-up list or enter the desired angle directly into the field.

4. The image should rotate.

5. The Rotate Tool [R] found in the tool bar can produce similar results.

Shearing or Skewing in Illustrator

1. Select the image using the Selection Tool found at the top corner of the tool bar [V].

2. On the top menu bar, go to the drop-down menu Window>Transform to open the Transform Palette. Click on the arrow next to the skew input field at the lower right of the palette.

3. Select the desired angle from the pop-up list or enter the desired angle directly into the field.

4. The image should be skewed.

5. The same effect can also be achieved using the Shear Tool found in the tool bar.

Flipping Images Horizontally in Illustrator

This is also called reflecting the image.

1. Select the image using the Selection Tool found at the top left corner of the tool bar [V].

2. On the top menu bar, go to the drop-down menu Window>Transform to open the Transform Palette. Click on the arrow in the upper right hand corner of the palette.

3. Choose Flip Horizontal

4. The image should be a mirror "reflection" of the original image.

5. This process can also be achieved using the Reflect Tool [O] found in the tool bar.

1

2

3

4

5

1. Select the image using the Selection Tool found at the top left corner of the tool bar [V].

    On the top menu bar, go to the drop-down menu Effect>Distort & Transform>Twist.

2. Enter the desired angle into the dialog box and press OK.

3. The image should twist.

4. To make the angle permanent, you need to expand its appearance. With the image selected, go to the drop-down menu Object>Expand Appearance on the top menu bar. Click OK in the dialog box that appears.

5. The image should now be permanently set at the selected angle.

35

1

2

Edit	Object	Type	Select	Filter
Undo Move				⌘Z
Redo				⇧⌘Z
Cut				⌘X
Copy				⌘C
Paste				⌘V
Paste in Front				⌘F
Paste in Back				⌘B
Clear				
Find and Replace...				
Find Next				
Check Spelling...				⌘I
Edit Custom Dictionary...				
Define Pattern...				
Edit Original				
Transparency Flattener Presets...				
Tracing Presets...				
Print Presets...				
Adobe PDF Presets...				
Color Settings...				⇧⌘K
Assign Profile...				
Keyboard Shortcuts...				⌥⇧⌘K

3

Edit	Object	Type	Select	Filter
Undo Move				⌘Z
Redo				⇧⌘Z
Cut				⌘X
Copy				⌘C
Paste				⌘V
Paste in Front				⌘F
Paste in Back				⌘B
Clear				
Find and Replace...				
Find Next				

4

5

6

7

You can turn an image into a pattern by repeating it.

1. Select the image using the Selection Tool found at the top left corner of the tool bar [V].

2. On the top menu bar, go to the drop-down menu Edit>Copy.

3. On the top menu bar, go to the drop-down menu Edit>Paste.

4. The copied image should be on the art board.

5. Move it close to the first image

6. Repeat steps 1 through 3 to get a third image.

7. Select all three images by holding down the shift key while selecting each image individually.

8. On the top menu bar, go to the drop-down menu Window>Align to open the Align Palette. Click the button Vertical Align Center to align the images.

9. Next click Horizontal Distribute Centers.

10. With the three images still selected, group them by going to the drop-down menu Object>Group on the top menu bar.

11. Copy the Groups images using steps 1 through 3. Repeat once more. You will have three groups of three images each.

12. Align the three groups using the Align Palette – Horizontal Align Center, then Vertical Distribute Center.

At some point you will want to add colors to your palette. Here is one way to do this.

1. On the top menu bar, go to the drop-down menu Windows>Swatches. This will open the Swatches Palette window. Select a color swatch. Click the Add New Swatch button in the lower right corner of the window next to the trashcan.

2. The Swatch Options window should appear. Change the color using the sliders at the bottom of the palette. You can change the mode using the drop-down Color Mode button. The global option will allow you to assign a color and change it globally in your document. Color type can be either Spot for PMS spot colors or Process for CMYK process colors.

3. When you finish creating the color swatch, type in a name for it and click the OK button.

4. Figure 4 shows the new orange swatch in the palette.

5. To add additional colors, repeat steps 1, 2, and 3.

Using A Limited Palette

A limited color palette helps you organize, harmonize, and set the mood for individual projects. A cool palette might consist of blues and grays; while a warmer palette would have more reds and yellows. If you are designing an image of a sunset, you won't need cool colors, so why add them to your palette?

Most of the examples shown in this book give the color palette used for both CMYK and RGB color modes.

0c	50m	80y	10k
30c	0m	30y	0k
30c	0m	10y	0k

223r	135g	65b
179r	221g	192b
174r	223g	228b

1. Select the image using the Selection Tool found at the top left corner of the tool bar [V].

   Select the fill square from the tool bar [K].

2. Fill the image by clicking on a color from the Swatches Palette Window.

Strokes or Outlines in Illustrator

1. Select the image using the Selection Tool found at the top left corner of the tool bar [V].

2. Select the stroke square from the tool bar [X].

3. Stroke the image by clicking on a color from the Swatches Palette window.

4. Change the size of the stroke by clicking on the blue arrow to the immediate right of the stroke input field.

5. Choose the designed stroke weight from the pop-up window or type in the desired weight.

Releasing a Compound Path in Illustrator

1

Object Type Select Filter
Transform	▶
Arrange	▶
Group	⌘G
Ungroup	⇧⌘G
Lock	▶
Unlock All	⌥⌘2
Hide	▶
Show All	⌥⌘3
Expand...	
Expand Appearance	
Flatten Transparency...	
Rasterize...	
Create Gradient Mesh...	
Slice	▶
Path	▶
Blend	▶
Envelope Distort	▶
Live Paint	▶
Live Trace	▶
Text Wrap	▶
Clipping Mask	▶
Compound Path	▶
Crop Area	▶
Graph	▶

Compound Path submenu:
Make	⌘8
Release	⌥⇧⌘8

2

3

4

Swatches — Orange

In order to work (color, stroke, drop shadow, etc.)
with the individual cells in a compound path,
you need to release the compound path.

1. Select the image using the Selection Tool
    found at the top left corner of the tool bar [V].

    Go to the drop-down menu Object>Compound
    Path>Release on the top menu bar.

2. Your image should look similar to Figure 2.
    Each individual shape that comprises the
    image is highlighted.

    These shapes are now independent of each other.

3. Deselect the image.

4. Select the image again and fill the top shape
    with a color.

5. With the shape still selected go to the drop-down
    menu Object>Arrange>Send to Back on the
    top menu bar.

5

Object Type Select Filter
Transform	▶
Arrange	▶
Group	⌘G
Ungroup	⇧⌘G
Lock	▶
Unlock All	⌥⌘2
Hide	▶
Show All	⌥⌘3
Expand...	
Expand Appearance	
Flatten Transparency...	
Rasterize...	
Create Gradient Mesh...	
Slice	▶
Path	▶
Blend	▶
Envelope Distort	▶
Live Paint	▶
Live Trace	▶
Text Wrap	▶
Clipping Mask	▶
Compound Path	▶
Crop Area	▶
Graph	▶

Arrange submenu:
Bring to Front	⇧⌘]
Bring Forward	⌘]
Send Backward	⌘[
Send to Back	⇧⌘[
Send to Current Layer	

6

6. The colored shape should now be behind all the other shapes.

7

7. Select one of the black shapes remaining and fill with a color.

8

8. Once a new color has been applied to the shape, your image should look similar to Figure 8.

9

9. Continue selecting the shapes and filling them with color to complete the image.

1. On the top menu bar, go to the drop-down menu Window>Layers to open the Layers Window. Create a new layer by clicking the New Layer button located in the lower right corner next to the trashcan.

2. Select the images or shapes you want to move to a new layer using the Selection Tool found at the top left corner of the tool bar [V].

3. With the images still highlighted, reselect the new layer (layer 2) by clicking the radio button next to the layer name.

4. On the top menu bar go to the drop-down menu Object>Arrange>Send to Current Layer. This will send all the shapes selected in step 2 to layer 2.

1

2

3

4

5

6

7

8

1. On the top menu bar, go to the drop-down menu Window>Swatches and Window>Gradient. This will open the Swatches and Gradient Palette windows.

2. Select the color you want to make into a gradient from the Swatches Palette and hold the left mouse button down while dragging the color swatch to the Gradient Palette window.

3. The swatch is placed on either the left or right hand swatch boxes on the gradient slider. The basic gradient should look similar to figure 3. You can adjust the gradient by moving the sliders and by dragging additional color swatches to the Gradient Palette window.

4. In the upper left hand corner of the Gradient Palette window will be the gradient you have just created. Select it and hold the left mouse button down while dragging it to the Swatches Palette.

   Note: The All Swatches button at the bottom of the Swatches Palette must be clicked in order to see regular colors together with gradients.

5. Your Swatch Palette should look similar to Figure 5.

6. Select the image you want to apply your new gradient to using the Selection Tool found at the top left corner of the tool bar [V].

7. Select your new gradient from the Swatches Palette. Your image should look similar to Figure 7.

8. To change the angle of a gradient, select the object containing the gradient, then type in a new angle in the angle input field in the Gradient Palette Window.

Adding a Drop Shadow in Illustrator

1. Select the image by using the Layers Palette. On the top menu bar, go to the drop-down menu Window>Layers to open the Layers Window. To select all the shapes on layer one, click the radio button located to the right of the layer name. Since you are adding a drop shadow, you want to select the bottom layer.

2. On the top menu bar, go to the drop-down menu Effect>Stylize>Drop Shadow.

3. A drop shadow dialog box should appear. Mode, Opacity, X and Y Offsets, Blur, Color, and Darkness are all variables that you can change to achieve different effects.

4. Click Preview to see what the shadow will look like. Once you are satisfied with it's appearance, click OK.

5. The image will have a shadow.

Using a Clipping Mask to Fill a Vector Shape with a Bitmap Image

1. On the top menu bar, go to the drop-down menu File>Place. Select the bitmap image you want to place using the Place Dialog Box, then click the place button. The bitmap image will be on the art board, but will be in front of the vector shape.

2. If it is not already highlighted, select the bitmap image using the Selection Tool found at the top left corner of the tool bar [V] On the top menu bar, go to the drop-down menu Object>Arrange> Send to Back. This will move the bitmap image behind the vector shape.

3. While holding down the shift key, select both the bitmap image and vector shape using the Selection Tool found at the top left corner of the tool bar [V]. On the top menu bar, go to the drop-down menu Object>Clipping Mask>Make.

4. The bitmap image will fill the vector shape.

Opening EPS Vector Images in Photoshop

Opening a EPS Vector in Photoshop

1. On the top menu bar, go to the drop-down menu File>Open. In the Open Window, find and select the EPS Vector file you want to open and click the Open button.

2. In the Rasterize Generic EPS Format Window, be sure to select a size that is large enough to fill your document. Because you are rasterizing the EPS, you will not be able to scale the image again without losing quality.

   Remember when working with pixel-based formats in Photoshop, it is always easier to scale down than up. Only EPS Vector files allow you to scale your images without loss of quality before embedding them into your Photoshop document. Not all EPS files are true vector-based objects.

Placing a EPS Vector in Photoshop

1. Be sure to have a blank or working document already open.

2. On the top menu bar, go to the drop-down menu File>Place. In the Open Window, find and select the EPS Vector file you want to place and click the Place button.

3. The EPS Vector will be placed in your blank document and will retain many of its vector-based qualities until it is rasterized. In Photoshop, this is called a Smart Object, since you can still edit it in its native format with a program such as Adobe Illustrator. Read more about Smart Objects in your Photoshop Web Help or the manual that accompanied your software.

1. Select the Magic Wand Tool [W] found in the tool bar.

2. Enter a value in the Tolerance field found near the top menu bar. The higher this value, the wider the range of colors that will be selected. You can change this value in accordance to the type of image you are using.

3. Select an area of the image.

Adding Color with the Paint Bucket in Photoshop

1. Select the Paint Bucket Tool [G] found in the tool bar.

   The Paint Bucket will use the color assigned to the foreground color box

2. Paint the object by clicking on it.

1. Select an area of the image using the Magic Wand Tool [W] found in the tool bar.

2. Double-click the Foreground Color box found at the bottom of the tool bar and open the Color Picker Palette. Select a color and click OK. The new color should display in the Foreground Color box in the tool bar.

3. On the top menu bar, go to the drop-down menu Edit>Fill. Select Foreground Color from the Fill Dialog Box and click OK

4. The section will be filled with the foreground color.

1. On the top menu bar, go to the drop-down menu File>New and create a new blank document.

2. On the top menu bar, go to the drop-down menu File>Open; find and select the EPS Vector file you want in your new document; click the Open button. On the top menu bar, go to the drop-down menu Select>All, then go to the drop-down menu Edit>Copy.

3. Go to the Layers Window in the new blank document made in step 1, and create a new layer by clicking on the New Layer button at the lower right corner next to the trash can.

4. On the top menu bar, go to the drop-down menu Edit>Paste. The vector shape copied in step 2 should now be on Layer 2. Repeat Steps 3 and 4 to add additional layers and images

5. To change the opacity of a layer, select the layer; click the arrow to the right of the Opacity field, and use the slider to manipulate the opacity.

Adding a Gradient with Photoshop Layer Styles

1. In the Layers Window, double-click the layer you want to add a style to. This will open the Layer Style Window.

2. In this window, select Gradient Overlay in the list of styles at the left of the window to open the Gradient Options Window.

3. Click the arrow at the right end of the gradient sample bar.

4. Choose a gradient from the pop-up menu.

5. Click the gradient swatch to open the Gradient Editor Window. Click on any of the color stop boxes to choose new colors.

6. In the Color Picker Window, select a new color and click OK

   You can also change the position of the color stop boxes by sliding them along the gradient bar

In addition to Adobe Illustrator and Photoshop, for which we have included instructional material within this book, there are many other software programs that allow you to use and edit vector-based images. Most of these programs are proprietary and must purchased, however, there are several open-source, freeware and shareware programs available for download over the internet. A good resource for information about both commercial and free software can be found at the following link:

http://en.wikipedia.org/wiki/List_of_vector_graphics_editors

There are several basic types of software programs with which vector images can be utilized. The following is a list of the most popular, by category.

Illustration:

Adobe Illustrator	www.adobe.com/products/illustrator
Corel Draw	www.corel.com
Macromedia Freehand	www.adobe.com/products/freehand
Microsoft Expression Suite	www.microsoft.com/expression

Page layout:

Adobe InDesign	www.adobe.com/products/indesign
Quark XPress	www.quark.com
Scribus	www.scribus.net

Web and web animation:

Adobe Flash	www.adobe.com/products/flash
Adobe Fireworks	www.adobe.com/products/fireworks

Photo editing:

Adobe Photoshop	www.adobe.com/products/photoshop
Paint Shop Pro	www.corel.com

Image editors:

Xara Xtreme	www.xara.com
Inkscape	www.inkscape.org

001

002

003

004

005

006

007

008

009

010

011 background

012

013

014

015

016

017

018

020

021

022

023

024

025 background

027

026

028

029

030

031

032

033

034

035

036

037

038

039

040

041

042

043

044

045

046

047

048

049

050

051

052

053

054

055

056

058

059

060

062

063

064

065 background

066

067

068

070

071

072

073

074

075

076

077

VECTORS

079

080

082

083

084

085

086

087

088

089

090

091 background

092

093

094

095

096

097

098

099

100

101

102

103

a
104

b
105

c
106

d
107

e
108

f
109

g
110

h
111

i
112

j
113

k
114

l
115

133

134

m 116
m 117
n 118
n 119
o 120
p 121
q 122

R 123
r 124
s 125
t 126
u 127

v 128
w 129
x 130
y 131
z 132

91

135

136

137

138

139

140

141

142

143

144 background

145

146

147 background

148

150

151

152

153

154

155

156

157 background

158

159

161

162

164

165

166 background

Aa Bb Cc Dd
167 168 169 170 171 172 173 174

Ee Ff Gg Hh Ji
175 176 179 180 181 182 183 184
177 178

Ji Kk Ll Mm Nn
185 186 187 188 189 190 191 192 193 194

Oo Pp Qq Rr
195 196 197 198 199 200 201 202

Ss Tt Uu Vv
203 204 205 206 207 208 209 210

Ww Xx Yy Zz
211 212 213 214 215 216 217 218

220

221

222

223

224

225

226

228

229

230

231

233

232

234

236

237

238

240

241

242

243

244

245

246

247

248

250

251

252

253

254

255

256

257

258

259

260

261

262 background

263

264

265 background

266

267

268

269